Copyrights and Contact

Written: by April D Williams

Editing: April D Williams

Design: April D Williams

Cover Photo: ZDivi

Copyright © 2015 by April D Williams (Ms.Infopreneur) and LyfeLyne Enterprize. LLC

ISBN-10: 0692407308
ISBN-13: 978-0692407301
ASIN: B00UQUCMUU

ALL RIGHTS RESERVED. NO PART OF THIS PUBLICATION MAY BE REPRODUCED OR USED IN ANY FORM OR BY ANY MEANS-GRAPHIC, ELECTRIC, OR MECHANICAL, INCLUDING PHOTOCOPYING, RECORDING, TAPING, OR INFORMATION STORAGE AND RETRIEVAL SYSTEMS-WITHOUT WRITTEN PERMISSION OF THE PUBLISHER AND COPYRIGHT PROPRIETOR THEREOF

FIRST PUBLISHED 2015 BY LYFELYNE ENTERPRIZE LLC

PHILADELPHIA, PA

HTTP://WWW.CHRONICLESOFLIVIN.COM

Table of Contents

7: Introduction

8: Get Prepared For Your Business

11: Chapter 1: Why Do You Want To Be An Entrepreneur?

14: Chapter 2: Know Your Talent and Passion

20: Chapter 3: Cause and Effect Desire Pushed Me Into Entrepreneurship

25: Chapter 4: Do It Right The First Time

33: Chapter 5: Get Your Body, Mind & Spirit Right!

40: Chapter 6: Don't Let Your Pass Dictate your Future

44: Chapter 7: How is your personal credit

50: Chapter 8: Budget Every Dollar You Make

55: Chapter 9: Take Good Notes

68: Chapter 10: Study Until You Understand

64: Chapter 11: Officially Legal

Lessons I Learned As An Entrepreneur

How I Can Save You From Costly Mistakes

By April D Williams

An imprint of LyfeLyne Enterprize LLC

Acknowledgements

Completing this book was a big task so I want to first thank God for giving me the knowledge and wisdom to gain strength and learn from my failures and mistakes. For letting me know clearly who's for me and against me and when it's the right time to release my talents and gifts. For bringing all my life experiences bad and good together for a wonderful new chapter of my life.

Thank you son, Zamir Deon Williams for reminding me to focus on one thing at a time and helping me to pen point my strongest gifts (sharing information and inspiring others.) You are wise beyond your years and I couldn't pray for a more intelligent, special, respectful, caring and understanding son. You motivate me to work harder every day. I'm so proud of you for completing your first book as well and I truly believe you will be the youngest #1 selling author in the world!:)

Thank you, Mom, Taffy for always being there when no one else was. For having patients with me even when you didn't understand me and probably thought I was crazy!:) Thanks for believing in me and investing in my dreams throughout the years. Also for always encouraging me to never give up.

To my brothers Kipp and Geoff thanks for your belief and investments in my dreams. For the great examples and advice you have giving me to raise a wonderful son.

I want to thank my aunts Ann and VV for being second moms to me. My God mother Ann for taking me many different places when I was young and teaching me the importance of reading. Opening me up to different things and also being another mom to me. Thank you Julia and DB for giving me motherly love and being there at times I needed help. To my cousins, friends, associates and sisters from another mother: Darlene, Cynthia, Shelly, Charlene, Raphael, Alexis, Buddha, Tonya, Orien, Aleah, Danielle, Yvonne, Lisa, Stacey, Marlaina, Charlotte, Rhonda, Tiffany, Karen Cecily, Tyra, Nikole, Kim, Ms.Carol Freeda. Natalie, Nina And my cousins and friends Keith, Herb, Vaugh, Tank, Dallas, Terry, Shock Shep, DJ Ran, Isaac, Ddub, Oliver, Ikie David, Carl, Mark, King Stro, Donte, Lewie. You have been there in one-way or another through my ups and downs encouraging me to keep going. Or supportive of my dreams and played an impacting role at some point in my life rather it was good or bad. And even though we might not talk everyday just know I appreciate all the lessons I've learned from you! I am who I am from them. Some of you were great practice in helping me recognize and enhance my talents and motivational gifts!:) To my God Kids Sakoyia and Ashae you have both in different ways allowed me to see the results of my patients, understanding and encouragement and for that I thank you.

My little cousins Desmond and Ryan thanks for your support and help in encouraging Zamir and being great young men for him to look up to. It has helped me in many ways. And thank you to my nieces and nephews and the rest of my cousins, family and friends that have supported and believed in all my crazy visions and dreams. Especially those who continued to believe the dreams before they saw the results. And those who always told me I would be a great motivational speaker and life coach. That's one of the things that inspired me to write this book and many more to come. It's so many people to name, I'm trying not to turn this into another book☺ but you all know whom you are and I love you all dearly! I have learned a lot from all of y'all in some kind of way. So don't be mad if I use one of your stories in the rest of my books!:) Funny after all I did no one saw this book coming!:)

Thanks Nannie and Aunt Barber for inspiring me through your words of wisdom and always telling me "It's going to be alright"

Most of all Thank You Grandpa for making me pull out the encyclopedias every time I asked you a question when I was young. And always encouraging me to gain knowledge and push harder with everything I do. Thanks for being interested in every activity I pursued and always telling me "You Can Do Anything You put Your Mind To"

Introduction

This book is dedicated to all the visionaries, ambitious dreamers, movers and shakers. Also this book is for people who never quit and accept every mistake and failure as an opportunity to grow and learn.

I was inspired to start writing books in 2007 although I dreamed of a title I could feel in my spirit it wasn't time to start writing. So I wrote the title down in one of my many idea books and just as I do with any other ideas I put it away. I truly believe timing is everything. Throughout the years I have started and completed many business ideas. That sometimes didn't go anywhere. Later I would realize; I was before the relevance of some of my ideas times.

My goal for this book is not just to share my mistakes and feed you great information for your life and business. But to help you identify your strengths, weaknesses and inspire you to grow, and stride for positive changes to become a better YOU!

Get Prepared For Your Business

Before you get started reading this book please get this list of supplies.

1. A pack of ink pens
2. 3 composition books one to write down the questions from this book with your answers.
   - The second one to journal your growth, ideas and new outlook on your life and business as you read.
   - The third book is to write your goals and bucket list moving forward. And don't be afraid to put a date by your goals that will hold you accountable.
3. A planner & Log book to keep up with important dates, contacts, conversations and meetings.
4. Calculator to keep up with your spending and budgeting.
5. Pack of folders to keep important documents, bills and papers organized. The more organized you are the better and smoother your business will run.
6. Calendar to keep important dates in front of you.

[LESSONS I LEARNED AS AN ENTREPRENEUR]

7. Post-its to post around as enforced reminders
8. Pocket composition or spiral book to jot everything you spend money on daily, in order to keep up with your spending habits.

9. 1 black or white large poster board paper, corkboard, canvas or you can use a cut out piece of cardboard box you are not using. This is the foundation to create your life and business vision board.

- Scissors to cut out your pictures and words for the vision board.
- A stick of glue, tapes thumbtacks or paste to hold your picture on the board.
- Stacks of old magazines or you can print pictures from the web. A couple of pictures of yourself and any family member you want to include. But remember this is your board so I suggest making a separate one that includes family and friends so you

won't lose track of your dreams and visions.
- Markers crayons or paint.

All of these items can be purchased from a dollar store or you might already have some. This is the first $15-20 you will invest in your business and prove to yourself that you are really ready for the entrepreneur journey! Save your receipts for taxes.

You can create your vision board as you are reading the book and keep adding throughout your life. Once you can visualize your dreams, visions and desires in front of you daily; you'll be surprised at how many accomplishments you will begin to check off. This book is one of many of my accomplishments from my vision board and idea book.

It's your board so make it exciting and creative and have fun with it!:)

Chapter 1

WHY DO YOU WANT TO BE AN ENTREPRENEUR?

(SBA.gov) An entrepreneur is a person who organizes and manages a business undertaking, assuming the risk for the sake of profit. An entrepreneur: Sees an opportunity. Makes a plan. Starts the business. Manages the business. Receives the profits.

In my opinion since I have been an entrepreneur majority of my life this is what entrepreneur means to me.

An Entrepreneur is a free spirit person blessed with a natural ability to lead people, dream big, has a gift of vision, has a good sense to see potential in others they don't sometimes see in themselves. They also have the ability to vision a cup that's half full to over flowing. Many Entrepreneurs are idealists before their time they currently live in and for this reason some are mistaken as crazy or weird! They work and fight hard for what they are passionate about even if others can't see the big picture as they do. They have thick skin to protect them from all the judgments and criticism they are continually faced with. They don't accept failure or quitting as an option! They regroup, re-plan and go at it harder then the last time. Entrepreneurs are some of the biggest risk takers in the world! They don't live by the status quo, they think outside the box and go against the grain. They are daredevils that will try almost anything once. Some entrepreneurs are feared because of their unbelievable drive and ambition. They are self-motivators, encouragers and great inspirers to others. A good entrepreneur can play the role of a leader and with out a second thought on an as needed bases be an inspirational team player.

They welcome a challenge; in fact many live for the challenge.

Most of all many Entrepreneurs are

misunderstood for their tenacity and perseverance to see what most would consider impossible become reality!!!

Now before we go any further I'll ask you again! "Why do you want to be an entrepreneur and do you have what it takes?"

Entrepreneurs are born with the natural ability to lead, tough skin to deal with skepticism and unexplainable passion, tenacity and drive to see a thing through even after numerous failures.

April D Williams

Reflection Moment:

1. Were you born to be an entrepreneur?
2. Are you prepared for the many challenges you will be face with?

http://www.Chroniclesoflivin.com/entrepreneur/

Chapter 2

KNOW YOUR TALENT AND PASSION

These are just a few of the many questions you need to ask yourself before you take off running. Many times people start a business without any plans in place no legal structure or business licenses. Some don't even have enough knowledge and experience in that particular arena. They just decide one day for various reasons that it would be nice to have a sports wear store because they like sports. Nevertheless, they have never worked in retail, don't know where the vendors and wholesale facilities are that sell sports wear merchandise and don't have a clue of the meaning units or bulk sale prices. Their only concern is how cool it would be to own a store that represents their hobby and become financially wealthy as a result.

Now I'm not saying you should not start a company based on your hobbies or likes. In fact that is the very thing you should do. Since your hobby is something you're passionate about. Your determination to see the business become reality will be genuine and the achievement will be greatly rewarding. It's just the same when you reward a child for doing good in school it gives them the desire to continue performing at their best.

It is also very important to know why you want to start your own business. Are you starting a business because your friend Bob has his own business? And he's doing great financially: travels a lot and has a beautiful house with many other materialistic things to identify his status. Then you have it all wrong! You have to think about how long Bob had his business: how many mistakes did he make, how much money did he lose, how much time daily did he put in before reaching that level of lifestyle?

Again these are the things people don't think about before they start a business. Therefore I want you to get in the mindset of thinking about your Startup as you read and learn.

Feed & Grow Your Purpose

Just as locating your passion and talents; knowing your purpose can give you even more clarity on what kind of business you can be successful at running. A lot of people think they know their purpose and start walking in it based off their talent and wonder why they do not get to far. You have to feed and grow your purpose in order for it to have a lasting impact on people. Set aside time daily to read, listen to webinars, go to seminars, look a tutorials etc. Anything you think you can gain more knowledge from to make you wiser about your purpose. The Internet is full of information. Google and You Tube are my best friends when I need to learn something. I have evolved from computer illiterate to building websites and video editing for clients. I have had some friends; books and classes give me a few pointers. Yet the Internet has been my main source of learning. If you are not sure what your talent or purpose is,

- **Sit down write a list of all the things that you do naturally and you are passionate about doing?**
- **Most of all, what are the obvious contributions to people's lives you make with little effort?**
- **What areas do people ask for your assistance and help with the most?**
- **What are your life experiences?**
- **What is your work experience?**

Then you will find your purpose! As a result you will also have transparent direction and guidance for your start up business and all its needed components.

Always keep in mind God created us all with and for a purpose. Therefore your purpose will be something that others can benefit from. For example all my life people have called on me for encouragement, motivation and inspiration.

My spirit was naturally wired with those components from youth. I was always a go-getter, very ambitious and failure has never been an option for me. So people would notice those attributes, get inspired and draw to me for encouragement and motivation while pursuing their dreams and visions. My life and work experience has allowed me to share knowledge and wisdom with people. Just as I am doing with this book!

I have worked in so many industries throughout my life thinking it was just to pay the bills. However, when I look back I realize my work experiences taught me customer service, sales, marketing, advertisement, management, finance, credit repair and the list goes on and on. Some people get bored or hate their jobs. Nevertheless, understand everything you do in life is meant to all come together and benefit your ultimate purpose on this earth. Even heart breaks, mistakes and struggles. So always search for the lessons and enhancements from your life journey to better understand who you are and why you exist?

Reflection Moment: Your Business

1. What are your natural talents and gifts?
2. What is your purpose?
3. What do people ask of you the most?
4. What kind of business do you want to start?
5. Do you have experience in this field?
6. Are you passionate about this line of work and industry?
7. Can you start it as a home base business or outside office?
8. Do you know your competitors have you done any research?
9. What skills have you gained from your life and work experiences that you can transfer to your new start up business?

Chapter 3

Cause and Effect

Desire Pushed Me Into Entrepreneurship

My first experience as an entrepreneur was over 20 years ago in my last year of high school. I attended the high school of Philadelphia Creative & Performing Arts for dance and drama. My intentions were to become a famous dancer, actor and model after watching the movie Fame with Irene Caria. At that time I lived in a bad urban area of Philadelphia. Although I got along well with the kids in my neighborhood, I had different dreams, goals and most of all my fashion was very diverse. I believe going to a high school filled with so many different cultures made me look at life and fashion differently. Also to further extend my outlook; my mother was a singer in a big band. She would take me to the studio with her often and allow me to watch her and my aunt's rehearsal for up in coming shows. In addition to keep me out of trouble and the streets my mother kept me involved in dance and modeling outside the school too! Therefore, all of that exposure to the entertainment business let me know that was the industry I would enjoy working in.

My last year of high school established the marketable gifts of creativity I honed. As my prom grew close I realized there wasn't one dress in the stores that caught my eyes. So I went to my mother since she also designed and made the band show costumes and asked for her help. Although she gave me some basic sewing lessons it wasn't enough time to learn before prom. And she was too busy to make my dress as well. So I designed my dream dress and gave it to a dressmaker to create. I also went on to design my girlfriends dress and we were among the best dress in the whole prom. Our dresses were made of leather and lace and in those days that was an uncommon mix of material. Those dresses were the start of my entrepreneurship as a fashion designer and tailor!

BE SURE OF YOUR BUSINESS, LACK OF KNOWLEDGE CAN BE COSTLY

After I designed the dresses; I went on to get my degree in Fashion Design and Tailoring. While attending school I started making clothes for myself. Since they were so unique people would stop me and ask where did I buy my outfit? I would tell them, "I made it" and $Ching $Ching they ask for my number and if could I make them an outfit? As a result, it was history in the making. I found myself sewing for many people staying up all hours of the night, sometimes getting as little as 3 hours of sleep. Now I was a young lady making money on my own with plenty of energy, drive and ambition to go with my talent.

I know you want me to get right to the information of starting your business; actually I am doing that! I am telling you my story to make you understand why and how you can identify what business you would be good at building. How it could make you feel when you're building it and what the response could be from others.

Now here's where I get back to the question I asked you in the beginning of this chapter and why? At that time, you would think because I had a stabled clientele, I should have had a lot of money in the bank. Or, raised enough money after at least 5 years of my 11 years of sewing to get my own boutique that I dreamed of. Nope! Although, at the time my talent and reputation had grown in a positive way, in fact I even had distinctive labels inserted in my client's clothes. But I was missing the most important tools; legal company name, license, business bank account and tax ID etc.

Have you ever wondered why a celebrity can be so rich one year and broke the very next year? That's because successful entrepreneurs, businesses and artists make it while only using 20-30% of their talents and gifts. The other percentages are: work ethics, skills, integrity, relationships, knowledge, preparation and character all mixed in a pot to perform great business. So pay attention to your life, strengths and weakness until you figure out how to balance it all for your benefit. Never move on emotions, they will make you create the worst mistakes. Always make decisions with a clear head then you will be more accepting of the results and understanding of the tweets you need to make in your plan.

Reflection Moment:

1. What's your truth?
2. Know what you don't want to do and what you love to do?
3. What does your gut tell you?
4. Listen to what feels right and it will lead you to what's right for you!
5. Don't be afraid of failure figure out the lesson in every mistake and failure.
6. Once you learn the lesson you will never make the same mistake again!

http://www.chroniclesoflivin.com/blog

Chapter 4

Do It Right The First Time

When I started my fashion design business there were not a mass of affordable personal computers available for sale. Cell phones were just becoming accessible to the public and Facebook, Twitter and Youtube C.E.O.s were probably babies or not born yet! Which means Google Search wasn't even a thought in the universe. Therefore you had to promote your business the old school way, by word of mouth. Although we had libraries, I was young and only concerned with creating and making money! My mother had no knowledge of running a business even though she designed clothing as well and performed at major events. She was also ignorant to the steps it took to form a professional business or company.

Consequently this is a perfect example of the difference between making money from your hobby vs. business. Just think of the possibilities if my mother and I would have had someone to take the time to teach us how to use our design and sewing talents to create a reputable business. Who knows we could have had an awesome mother and daughter clothing line and boutique.

You see how easy your talent and gifts can be taken for granted unconsciously? Also how important it is for you to learn as much as you can about the business you are about to start and all the needed tools to make it look and run professionally!

IMAGE AND ATTITUDE IS EVERYTHING!

DRESS THE PART

Now that I shared one of my business downfalls with you, you can understand what gives me the expertise to write this book. Hopefully I can save you from these very same mistakes. Always remember if you don't know any better, you can't do any better. And think about how you see yourself because that will project how others see you. In other words Image is 80% of your business. Think about a corporate job interview with a young man walking in with unruly hair, sagging pants and all his tattoos exposed. Then think about the young man from the same part of town coming in with a clean cut, neatly dressed with a respectful confident attitude. The young man inappropriately dressed could very well be better for the job. But he risked his opportunity to prove it because he didn't present a respectful looking image. No matter how you feel about that case in point, it's the truth! However, if the industry you're applying for is driven from unprofessional dress code (music or tattoo artist for example), then a dress down style will be appropriate.

CHANGE YOUR WAYS

LEARN HOW TO BE MULTILINGUAL

Throughout my time of working as an entrepreneur I have met countless people blessed with exceptional gifts and talents. I knew in my heart they should be further in their business industry and financially set. However they were stuck in a clientele comfort zone. It wasn't just the fact they continued to serve people they knew or was acquainted with in some ways from their social circle. On the contrary they acted and presented themselves and their business in the same way for every potential client. As a result they attracted the same type of business over and over, which caused a staggering income. Although they would have a streak of luck from time to time and land a different type of client it wouldn't last. Since they were unwilling to alter their approach according to the client's conformability.

Let me explain what I am trying to get across to you. I grew up in the hood as people call it today. Nevertheless I didn't go to my neighborhood school and I have worked in different industries and lived in different states. Throughout my many changes of environment I was afforded the ability to meet and experience people of different cultures, status and race. This allowed me to observe and find there are many ways to view and communicate with people. And there are also many ways to intimidate and disinterest people by your presents alone.

SHORT STORY

I was a sales manager over a 200 plus apartment unit for a real estate investment group. My property manager had a few degrees in business while mines was in fashion with sales, mortgage and paralegal experience at that time. Part of her job description was to collect the rent, keep the property clean and in ordered. There were a few unruly tenants that weren't paying the rent and were suspected of selling drugs.

The property manager dressed seductive and had multiple relationships with some of the tenants despite the fact she and her husband lived on the premise. Consequently the tenants didn't value her and that made her job a difficult task. I also lived on the premise with my young son except; I kept to myself, dressed in the appropriate attire and treated everyone with respect. For that reason, I was able to talk to the unruly tenants without chaos and resolve the problem. Although I myself grew up around a lot of drug dealers I didn't present myself in that fashion. And since I always carried myself and approached them in a professional and respectful manner regardless of the situation. They not only returned the respect but they cleaned up the trash that surrounded their apartment unit.

So you see how altering your identity for clients has its advantages with getting the results you need and want! While the tenants were a problem they still were customers that was suppose to pay for a service. And I felt it would cost the apartment unit more if I had approached them with a street mentality just because I grew up in that same environment. Not only would we have lost rent payments but also they could have trashed the apartment and we would have to pay for damages plus lost of rent.

However from my professional approach and civilized conversation without judgment the tenants paid the rent. Also agreed to stop the suspicious traffic from entering their unit and to keep their surroundings clean of liter. Problem solved!

Lessons Learned

Since this is a book to teach you how to start and run a business professionally. I felt that was a great story to share for the fact that whatever business you decide to build you never know a potential clients background just from appearance. Always try to be opened and non judgmental you never know who the potential client has relationships with. They could be Jay-Z cousin or Katie Perry's friend. Yet, if you are not professional in your appearance, attitude or approach it can cause you to lose out on a string of potential wealthy clients. That can change your business status overnight.

Reflection Moment:

1. **When You Look in The Mirror Who Do You See?**
2. **Are You Opened To Constructive Criticism?**
3. **Are You Willing To Change Your Ways?**
4. **Is Your Hygiene up to par?**

Chapter 5

Get Your Body, Mind & Spirit Right!

Before you start or open your business make sure these important things are in sequence, so you can function right. When things around you are unorganized, it is received as a bunch of noise. This can complicate hearing from your spirit, mind or body needs. Therefore, if we take the time to de-clutter our surroundings we will be more receptive to the needs to feed and strengthen every element of our soul.

Eating the right diet of food can make a huge difference in your energy and focus. Try to stay away from package foods with a paragraph of ingredients you cannot pronounce or never heard of.

Make sure you take time at the top of the day to pray, meditate and reflect on the things you have to be grateful for. Even if your life is not where you want it to be, you can be grateful for God allowing you to have another day to do better and be a better person. Get up a half hour earlier to exercise, stretch, or walk. Just make sure you do something to stay fit. Feed your mind positive thoughts that things can only get better, read inspirational books or start your day off listening to inspirational music. While your driving to work listen to an audio book or something that is motivating; that can teach you more about your purpose and business you are pursuing.

Who inspires me to want to do better and be better?

These are people that you can always draw positive energy from every time you are in their presents or you speak with them. They recognize your potential even when you do not and empower you to pursue your purpose even through your failures. You can call these people at your lowest point and they can make you view things from a different angle. Through conversation they can jump-start your spirit like a dying car battery. These are people who inspire you to push harder then ever. They are keepers in your journey!

Remember that saying? "Everybody can't go!" This means when you are on a journey to pursue your dreams and visions sometimes your closest friends and family members aren't supportive. Everybody won't be as excited as you are. Those are the people that will probably never be supportive through your building and creative state. But, they are always the first ones to brag and claim you as a cousin when the success comes!

Observe, listen and detach yourself from the doubters and haters. You need to distance yourself ASAP no matter who it is! You can still love them from a far. Even if it's your parents, if they are not supportive make sure you don't talk about your plans when they are around. Ask them about their well-being and life to keep them from putting doubt in your spirit. Since most of the time parents have the biggest impact on our life.

Always surround yourself with like-minded people to stay encouraged. And find a mentor, physically or virtually. Listening to haters and doubters can cause you to stop before you even start.

Focus and Discipline

While everything I listed is important, without these two factors you will never get to the others successfully. As I always say, "Your time is very valuable." So learning how to plan it out and sticking to it, is the key. You must determine the distractions in your life and learn to control them.

Example: Once my son is off to school I work until a set break/lunch time. Since I work from home a lot, if I get drowsy I do not take naps I fight through by going to the door to get a little air or get out the chair and do a few stretches. I work a full 9-5 day and sometimes longer. I create a monthly goal list, weekly To-Do and agenda list and check off each accomplishment daily. I do not have a TV in my office. When I am writing or reading I make sure the TV is off or I am in a separate room with no TV. If I get a phone call while I am working from home I will not answer it. I will listen to the voice mail on break or when I am done and return calls then, unless it is a business call.

Sure it takes a while to discipline yourself when no one is looking over your shoulder. Yet so many people complain about being at a job with someone looking over their shoulder. So you need to make up your mind; do you want to be controlled or do you want to be in control? You can't have it both ways unless you are a part time entrepreneur and full time employee.

Most people think when you are an entrepreneur/business owner; you have more free time on your hands. In some cases that is true, depending on your type of business. But with every start up you will work longer hours until your company can run it self. Even then you have to stay on top of things. Since in many cases success can go just as fast as it comes.

Take notes from Hollywood celebrities falling off and big businesses closing down. Never underestimate your competitors even when you're in the lead. They can pass your status when you least expect it. Stay passionate and hungry with every opportunity. And continue to learn new things to be prepared for any industry changes.

Never Stop Learning

Failure Creates Tenacity and Strengthens You, While Shaping Your Character. Mistakes Gives You Knowledge, Teaches You To Think Wisely And Enhances Your Discernment.

April D Williams

http://www.Chroniclesoflivin.com/life-coach/

Chapter 6

Don't Let Your Past Dictate your Future

Some people are paralyzed with dreams and visions locked inside of them. They have great ideas of ways to get wealth by benefiting others in a major way. Nevertheless they doubt themselves because of a dark pass or become products of their environment. Maybe they are a recovering drug addict, dealer, prostitute or abused victim. And because of their pass they can't see a bright future. Since they still associate with people that haven't gone much further then they have.

I'm here to tell you this book is especially for you! I have watched so many talented people lose out on the wealth their God given gifts could have made room for. I don't know your religion but I know that you wouldn't have visions and dreams if; they were not meant to be used! Sometimes you have to encourage and motivate yourself and others will start feeding into that positive energy and begin to cheer you on.

While there will always be haters in your mist. There are also people in your surroundings that are seeking someone they can look up to and inspire them to gain the courage to pursue their dreams and visions also. Guest what that someone may just be you!

At the end of the day people will forget about your past. If you focus on using those experiences to share with others in order to help them from making the same mistakes. Just like I am doing with this book.

You have to understand that everyone has made mistakes in his or her life or will in his or her future. It is all about the lessons you learn and actions you take after, that really matters!

Most importantly remember when you want better you have to surround yourself with people that are doing better. And learn from them. You don't have to forget your friends or where you came from. But we only get one life and there is a big world out there with many people and cultures for you to meet and explore.

Stepping out of your comfort zone is the only way to grow and change your mindset to become a better you.

Inspiration

Turning a dark past into a bright future

I know a man that sold drugs in his pass and use the drug money to pay for a college education. A few years later he was locked up and did some time in prison. Once he was released he went on to get a great job. After working for a few years he decided to turn a building he purchase into a restaurant. Since he didn't have any former restaurant experience he went to culinary arts school to get his cooking/chef certification. Afterwards he went on to hire staff that was familiar with the industry in order to run a professional and successful business.

While I don't applaud the drug dealing part this man is proof that you can use your past experiences to paint a bright and positive future.

When he was a drug dealer he was an entrepreneur by right since he was the boss, distributing and selling product to people through his street staff. So at that time he was managing, supervising, budgeting and giving customer service all at the same time. Even though we all know that wasn't a positive business to run. The man will be able to utilize his past entrepreneurship and transfer all of those skill sets to run his current business.

See how easy you can use your mistakes and past to work towards a positive outcome. The same man that once ran a negative business is now helping people take care of their families by working for his establishment. Your future can be bright too. It is just a matter of

getting out of your own way and looking in front of you not behind.

Chapter 7

How Is Your Personal Credit?

I started to talk about your credit earlier but I really didn't want that to discourage you if it's not "A" status. Since credit is what stops a lot of people from pursuing their dreams. I will be the first to tell you please don't let that be an excuse for you. So many people have credit issues, including me. Yet if I chose to focus on that you would not be reading and learning from this book right now. Sure credit is something we need to prove we are worthy of loans and investing in. But even rich people like Donald Trump had his share of credit problems. I lost count with how many times he filed bankruptcy. And it still didn't stop him from pursuing production of one of the most watch TV reality shows "**The Apprentice.**" However, Donald continues to invest in big real estate deals. I don't even think the man had a moment of shame although he was all over the news and TV being criticized about his credit. Nevertheless, he walks with his head up high and still manages to be respected by many.

If you are facing credit issues pull your credit from each one of the credit bureaus (Trans Union, Equifax and Experian)

You are allowed 1 free credit report per year. So go on their websites and get started.

http://www.equifax.com/CreditReportAssistance/

http://www.transunion.com/personal-credit/credit-management/credit-monitoring.page

http://www.experian.com/consumer-products/credit-report.html

Once you pull your credit, if you see something on there you don't agree with call them and request a dispute form, fill it out and mail it to the creditor noted on your report and a copy to the credit bureau. The company has up to 30 - 45 days to get back to you with proof of the original paper work you signed for their services or product. If they don't get back within that time they have to remove that account off your credit. If an account is past 7 years and it's still reporting you have the right to dispute that too. By law a bad account/charge off is suppose to drop off your credit since by then their insurer has paid them. If you have debt that's 3 years or less work on paying it down. It will bring your score up! Start with paying the smallest bill off first so you won't get overwhelmed. If your debt is charged off or passes 3 years it's best to negotiate a 40%-50% payoff or dispute it. Since it's charged off, paying it is consider bringing bad debt current and it can drop your score lower then it is. The only debts you can't dispute are government, student loans or taxes. Although in some cases you can call and negotiate a lower payoff for as low as 40% of the original amount due.

Most importantly once you pay please don't forget to request a paid in full or payoff receipt/letter from the creditors and send a copy to the bureaus. Some creditors won't update your credit so it's up to you to follow up!

As I said, this book is about providing you tools, tips and resources to help you start your entrepreneur journey. So I'll give you a few more bullet points about credit and save the rest for another book.

Always keep 3 lines of revolving credit opened. This includes credit cards, car notes, mortgage, and lines of bank credit or student loans. Not cell phone, utilities, and cable bills although they could be used as an alternate credit source if you're purchasing a house or car. But that's for another book.

Make sure one of the lines of credit is a least $1000 if you don't have that right now you can work toward it. The other 2 can be below that amount.

- A good way to build credit is to take your own money $300-$500 and go to your bank and ask them to put your money towards a secure credit card.

- Never spend more then 40% of your credit card limit, even if you pay the bill on time, the more you spend the credit bureau will view you as more of a risk. Paying on time towards a lower balance due increases your score. The higher your score the more you qualify for.

- Apply for a credit card like a first Premiere, Capital One, or First Progress. Yes these cards make you pay a fee but if you have bad debt it's a good way to get back on track. Again remember keep the card under 50%

- A secured credit card is a credit card that requires a security deposit. **Secured credit cards** are generally for individuals whose credit is damaged or who have no credit history. Your credit line will represent anywhere from 70% - 100% of your security deposit. Depending on the credit card issuer, some secured credit cards require a deposit for a limited time such as one year. If your history with the credit card is good, the credit card issuer may extend your line of credit or offer you an unsecured card. An unsecured credit card is one that does not require a security deposit. **Unsecured credit cards** are intended for individuals with good or excellent credit.

Those are just a few tips you can apply to your personal and business credit to get you on track. I'll give you more tips in my next book about credit.

RECAP:

- Visit and study all suggested business websites
- Register for any seminars, webinars or classes that could help your business
- Attend any beneficial networking events, prepared with business cards
- Pull your free credit report from all 3 credit bureaus
- Check for any errors and study to see what improvements you can make
- When paying debt start with the smallest
- Keep all credit card balances below 50%
- Apply at your bank for a unsecured credit card or for bad credit a secured card to use your money for business and personal credit building
- Always keep at least 3 lines of good credit and more or work up to that
- Dispute or negotiate for lower payoffs on all charge offs or 7 year old trade lines on your credit

Chapter 8

Budget Every Dollar You Make

Have you ever got to the end of the week or month and said to yourself "Where did all my money go?" Well you're not the only one. You will be surprise how much money you spend on unnecessary things throughout the week. One cup of coffee turns into a cup of coffee everyday. Or one trip to your favorite lunch place turns into 15 times a month. That $1-5-10 adds up. Although it seems little and innocent at the top of the month by the end of the month your sitting there with a sad face!

Budgeting Tricks

When I was a loan officer, yeah I worked in that industry for years too and still have a notary license. My clientele was 80% bad credit people this is why I'm able to teach you so much about credit. I would find out their spending habits and challenge them to carry a small journal in their pocket or purse and write everything they buy even if it's paying 0.75 to put air in your car tire. At the end of the week I would make them total their spending, look at the total then look at the list and note what was priority and what was want? Once they got a clear picture of where their money was going they were willing to change their mindset and become more frugal with their finances, to save more money. Another one is going in the market or store for one thing and coming out with 5 more added that wasn't on your list. In this case you should always keep inventory of when you run out of something and write it down or store it in your task section of your phone. And most of all never go to the market hungry!

Another way to control your spending is don't carry much cash on you the more cash you have on hand the more you will spend. I personally keep $10-20 hidden in my car for emergencies and $10-20 in cash on me. Of course I still carry my bankcards but most of the time I try not to use them unless I have a planned shopping day, lunch meeting or entertainment event to attend. If you have spending habits that are just flat out horrible; I suggest paying yourself a weekly cash allowance. Leave your debit card in the house for 21 days to break that habit. Once you spend the weekly cash allowance, do not get more out the bank until your next weekly allowance day. This will teach you to be more conscious of your spending. If that doesn't work for you set up the envelop method: buy a box of envelops from the dollar store, then use a separate one for each bill. For ex: gas, electric, cable, phone etc. Then write entertainment or weekly spending. To take it steps further divide the allowance by the day. Ex: $20-Monday, $75- Friday, you get the point! Just try different formats until one works for you.

When you have your own business, especially a start up it is best to make sure you take 10% donation for God/church, good cause or a charity. I truly believe in what you do will come back to you! Take 10% or more to invest in a savings, stock or retirement account. Then make sure all bills (business and living expenses) are paid and you pay yourself last. Pay all your bills by priority and whatever is left is spending money for the week or month according to how you get paid. Afterward, break your spending money up in equal amounts ($10, $20 or more per day leading to your next pay. It might sound like a small amount but unless you have a planned lunch meeting or shopping trip for a day then you really shouldn't need that much money to survive daily.

I know it sounds like a lot of structure but these are great habits to embrace. Also it teaches you how to value money and allow budget consciousness to grow in you. Now the amounts I used for example can be whatever you feel is comfortable for you. Although, rather I have thousands or millions I just don't believe in spending money senselessly everyday just because you have it. How many celebrities and wealthy people have been in the news because of going broke? They were doing the very thing I'm trying to convince you to be disciplined against.

If your office or business is outside of the home, it would be wise to pack a lunch. Or if you have a refrigerator and small microwave in your office you can stock it every week with food and drinks. Packing lunch should not be just for kids. Make it exciting, team up with a co-worker or friend and pack each other's lunch. This will make it fun and interesting, waiting to see what you are going to eat for lunch. Make sure you give each other a list of your favorite foods and things you are allergic to. Trust me it will save you a ton of money. This way you are just spending money on business lunch meetings and if you keep those receipts, at tax time you can write those business lunch dates off and get reimbursed. Just think about it for a minute and do the math. Let's say the average person spends up to $10+ a day eating lunch and snacks while working outside the home. 10x5=50x4=200x12=2400. So you'll be saving $2400 a year just for taking lunch to work. That's $2400 that could be spent on advertisement, marketing or new equipment for your business. Do you understand now how important it is to be budget conscious?

One of the most important things about budgeting is practicing the 40/60 rules. Making sure your bills don't exceed 60% of what you make. Work to save at least 3-6 months of your monthly billing amount in your bank for an emergency cushion and ask your banker for the best interest building savings product.

OK LET'S RECAP:

- **Control your spending, budget and divide your finances as soon as you make profit.**
- **Carry a small spending journal with you daily**
- **Save 10% or more, and give 10% of your finances to charity**
- **Pay yourself an allowance after your priorities are paid.**
- **Carry small amounts of cash**
- **Pack lunch or stock your office refrigerator weekly**
- **Keep a small amount of cash in a hidden area of your car for emergencies**
- **Keep or get your billing budget down to no more then 60% of your profits.**
- **Save 3-6 months of your monthly billing amount in a interest driven savings account**

Chapter 9

Take Good Notes

The Start Of It All

1. Fictitious Name, EIN Tax Identification
2. Business Structure: A Limited-Liability-Partnership
3. Nonprofit Organization
4. Corporation-S Corporation-Cooperative
5. Sole Proprietorship
6. Business License/Trade Mark/Insurance

I know your saying ok this is starting to look a little complicated. I thought the same thing when I first started learning about all it takes to run a professional legit business. However these are the first steps you need to take before anything else. Nevertheless I am here to make things a little easier for you to understand. Like I wish someone did for me at the beginning of my journey.

Here are some brief descriptions of corporate structures:

- Sole Proprietorship - A sole proprietorship is the most basic type of business to establish. You alone own the company and are responsible for its assets and liabilities. Be careful with this form because if someone sues you they can sue for your personal assets.

- Limited Liability Company - An LLC is designed to provide the limited liability features of a corporation and the tax efficiencies and operational flexibility of a partnership.

- Corporation - A Corporation is more complex and generally suggested for larger, established companies with multiple employees.

- Partnership - There is several different types of partnerships, which depend on the nature of the arrangement and partner responsibility for the business.

- S Corporation - An S Corporation is similar to a C corporation but you are taxed only on the personal level.

- Nonprofit Organization - (NPO, also known as a non-business entity) is an organization that uses its surplus revenues to further achieve its purpose or mission, rather than distributing its surplus income to the organization's directors (or equivalents) as profit or dividends.

https://www.sba.gov/category/navigation-structure/starting-managing-business/starting-business/choose-your-business-stru

Chapter 10

Study Until You Understand

Fictitious business name AKA "Doing Business As" Name Registering your DBA is done either with your county clerk's office or with your state government, depending on where your business is located. There are a few states that do not require the registering of fictitious business names.

https://www.sba.gov/content/register-with-state-agencies

Federal Licenses & Permits:

Certain businesses, like ones that sell alcohol or firearms; require a federal license or permit.

State Licenses & Permits: Some states have requirements for specific businesses.

Virtually every business needs some form of

license or permit to operate legally. However, licensing and permit requirements vary depending on the type of business you are operating, where it's located, and what government rules apply.

To help you identify the specific licenses or permits your business may need, use SBA.Gov's Permit Me tool. Simply enter your zip code and business type to view a list of the licenses or permits you'll need, together with information and links to the application process.

https://www.sba.gov/content/what-state-licenses-and-permits-does-your-business-need

Obtain Your Federal Business Tax ID:

An Employer Identification Number (EIN) is also known as a Federal Tax Identification Number, and is used to identify a business entity. Generally, businesses need an EIN.

https://www.sba.gov/content/obtain-your-federal-business-tax-id-ein

Trade Name VS Trademark

How are trade names and trademarks different? Does a trade name afford any legal branding protection? Can your trade name be the same as your trademark?

Simply put, a trade name is the official name under which a company does business. It is also known as a "doing business as" name, assumed name, or fictitious name. **A trade name** does not afford any brand name protection or provide you with unlimited rights for the use of that name. However, registering a trade name is an important step for some – but not all – businesses.

A trademark is used to protect your brand name and can also be associated with your trade name. **A trademark** can also protect symbols, logos and slogans. Your name is one of your most valuable business assets, so it's worth protecting.

An important reason to distinguish between trade names and trademarks is that if a business starts to use its trade name to identify products and services, it could be perceived that the trade name is now functioning as a trademark, which could potentially infringe on existing trademarks.

Patents Protect Your Inventions

Here's the deal: If you invent or discover a new and useful "process, machine, manufacture, or composition thereof" you can apply for a federal patent to protect your invention from being used by others without your permission.

- There are three basic types of patents:

- Utility patents protect machines and industrial processes and last for 20 years.

- Design patents protect designs of manufactured items and last for 14 years.

- Plant design patents (rare) protect new plant varieties and last for 20 years.

Business Liability Insurance

Two common types of liability insurance – Comprehensive General Liability and Professional Liability- each protect your business from different types of claims that may be brought against you.

Comprehensive general Liability insurance is usually limited to claims of bodily injury or other physical injury or damage to property. Often, General Liability insurance is offered in a package with Property coverage to protect against accidents on your premises or at other locations where you normally conduct business.

If you provide professional services such as accounting, computer consulting, or medical care, Professional Liability insurance is a critical coverage. Professional Liability (sometimes called Errors and Omissions coverage) protects your business against claims of alleged negligent acts, errors or omissions in the performance of your professional services. This is important because Professional Liability claims can be extremely large as compared to General Liability claims.

https://www.score.org/blog/2010/julie-brander/planning-finding-best-small-business-insurance

Chapter 11

Officially Legal

What's Next?

I am sure you're thinking; ok what could possible be needed after all of that is set up? Again I'm giving you the tools that's needed for you to set up a professional looking and functioning business. That doesn't mean you need every last tool in this book or you have to get them all in place before you start. You might not have the money for everything right now and I don't want that to stop you from your dream. So at the end of the book I will give you the first few things you should have in place before you start making moves. I'm saving the summarized list for the end to assure you read, everything so you won't just start with the summary tool list and never put all the other steps in place.

This chapter will go over more things that you need to have in place in order to be professional and efficient with your business.

Get Assistance and Protect Your Company

When you start a new business you need help most of the time. Again depending on your type of business. And how you present yourself and business ethics at the beginning will leave a lasting impression on your employees. Therefore be as professional as you can by having everything in order. That will set the pace for the level of respect all new hires will give you and your company.

This means even if they are a friend or family member make them go through the same hiring process as a stranger. Make them fill out an application, contract agreement or whatever legal binding documentation your industry requires.

There are some free sample and paid templates websites that supply all the

professional legal forms, applications, contracts, agreements and more. These sites will help you save on cost to avoid expensive lawyer fees until you profit enough to hire one on an as needed base.
https://www.rocketlawyer.com

http://www.legalcontract.com/

http://formswift.com/

Microsoft Office offers free templates that can be a great help to keep your business looking professional on a budget. They have templates to keep your business organized like planners, agendas, budget sheets and spreadsheets. Also they offer marketing and advertising templates like: business cards, brochures, flyers and so much more. Templates are formatted for all of Microsoft Suite versions.

https://templates.office.com/Templates

Here are a few sites that can help you with creating a Logo and brand for your company.

Branding your business is one of the most important ways for people to remember you. Take Nike sneakers, you can see their logo anywhere alone and know that it represents Nike sneakers. So be very careful with creating your brand.

http://www.freelogoservices.com/

http://www.logogarden.com/

http://www.creativemarket.com

http://www.cooltext.com/logos

Here are some reasonable price online printing stores for all your marketing and advertising materials.

http://www.uprinting.com/
http://www.vistaprint.com/
http://www.avery.com/avery/en_us/

Another way to cut on cost is to hire college interns that are studying to obtain a degree in your industry. They work for free in order to gain a great recommendation letter from you. So this is a win-win situation.

Building a website can be done a month or so before your business is opened. I will go more indebt about Internet appearance in my next book. Until then here a few great free website platforms for you to learn. When your business starts making money then start paying for a package so they can remove their brand ads off your site.

http://www.wordpress.com

www.wix.com

http://www.weebly.com

www.homestead.com

http://www.web.com

You can also hire Virtual-Assistants for low cost to help you keep things on tasks.

http://www.odesk.com/Virtual-Assistants

http://www.answerconnect.com

http://www.virtualassistantfromphilippines.com

If you are on a real tight budget Fiverr has all kinds of services to offer. And you can read freelancers ratings to make a good conscious decision when picking whom to try.

http://www.fiverr.com

And most of all you must have social pages to stay connected with clients and promote your businesses. Just monitor your time on them.

www.YouTube.com

www.FaceBook.com

www.Twitter.com

www.meetup.com

www.linkedin.com

www.istagram.com

Here's a great time management website. It really keeps me on track.

www.rescuetime.com

Business Websites To Keep Up With

When you start a business you need as many resources to help you stay a head of your competitors and feed you as much knowledge as you can get. Since there are so many websites out there that focus on business. It can get over whelming as to which one gives the most relevant information you can use for your type of business.

So I am going to give you a few one-stop shops websites:
I've have noted the **SBA** http://www.SBA.gov links a few times in the prior pages.

About – SBA Since it's founding on July 30, 1953, the U.S. Small Business Administration has delivered millions of loans, loan guarantees, contracts, counseling sessions and other forms of assistance to small businesses. SBA was officially established in 1953, but its philosophy and mission began to take shape years earlier in a number of predecessor agencies, largely as a response to the pressures of the Great Depression and World War II.

I have learned so much from the SBA once you go on their website make sure you signup if you haven't already. Hopefully you have from the links I provided to you earlier. I purposely waited to tell you why I utilize them as much as I do. Since I wanted you to take the first steps in learning how to research business information from the leads I provided.

In the business world many don't like to share information. The SBA offers a lot of free seminars for small business across the country. They also have plenty of free learning tutorial videos and webinars on their website.

It would be a great benefit to you to go to their free classes and seminars some cost a small fee but if your able to make those too it would help you just as well. You can take advantage of networking with like-minded people or making a good business connection.

Another site to keep up with is **Dun & Bradstreet** http://www.dnb.com/ they have been around for years and they provide a good way for you to build your business credit and help you to understand how your credit can work for you and against you.

About - D&B (NYSE: DNB) is the world's

leading source of commercial information and insight on businesses, enabling companies to Decide with Confidence® for more than 173 years. Today, D&B's global commercial database contains more than 225 million business records. The database is enhanced by D&B's proprietary DUNSRight® Quality Process, which provides our customers with quality business information. This quality information is the foundation of our global solutions that customers rely on to make critical business decisions.

The Better Business Bureau can allow you to keep up with your competitors to see what customers are saying about them you can also take advantage of any training they may have for you and your business.

About - BBB www.bbb.org helps consumers identify trustworthy businesses, and those that aren't, through more than 4 million BBB Business Reviews. BBB sets standards for and evaluates the practices of thousands of charities so that donors know where their money is going. BBB coaches businesses on ethical behavior and how to build stronger, more trusting relationships with their customers.

About - U.S. Chamber of Commerce
https://www.uschamber.com/ is another great source to learn from, network through and get involved with.

The U.S. Chamber of Commerce is the world's largest business organization representing the interests of more than 3 million businesses of all sizes, sectors, and regions. Our members range from mom-and-pop shops and local chambers to leading industry associations and large corporations. They all share one thing in common—they count on the Chamber to be their voice in Washington, D.C.

If you are serious about your business then

those are just a few sites to get started looking into. Even if you don't sign up as a member or for their services, there is so much free information that you can learn from them to help you in major ways. When you are just starting a new business I don't suggest spending a lot of money on memberships or services that can't make you "Now Money." Yet I do expect you to take advantage of their free resources. In order that when you do start making money you will know which services is worth paying for first that you feel will help your business grow. Just think of it as business window-shopping!

Through the years I have learned so much from Google.com search bar and Youtube.com. While others spend hours on Facebook or Twitter. I spend hours searching reading and learning through Google and You Tube. I feel like I should get an advertisement check from them right now for all the promotion I've given them in this paragraph! Seriously when you have a business you should always be opened to learn more. No matter how old you get; even in your personal life. That's how you become wiser, and make better choices and decisions as a result of the knowledge you gain. So make Google search and You Tube your friends and teachers to search for any other association, organizations or membership services that can help you in the future. Also search for seminars, webinars and tutorial just put your industry name in and click on the links that interest you; you'll be surprise how much you learn in a short time.

How To Use My Business Name

Now that you have all of your company documents it's time to open your company bank account. Before picking a bank call them or look at their website to see who has the best deal for start up companies/small

businesses. Ask questions about tools they have for business, see how their customer service department treats you? These are some of the most important people you're going to have to deal with since they will be holding your money.
So read reviews and pick wisely which one is best for you.

Ask about their online budgeting, accounting or bookkeeping programs. How their over draft protection works and do they charge for a checking account etc. Some banks give you free access to Quick Books. This is great accounting software to help keep your spending and employee payments in order, along with vendors and clients financial deposits.

Start Your Own Business with These Key Considerations

Read these useful tips to get an idea about what sorts of questions you should be asking yourself as you consider setting up your own business:

- Get everyone involved in setting goals and objectives.
- Learn all you can about your customers.

- Understand who your competitors are.
- Identify your strengths and weaknesses relative to opportunities and threats.
- Determine which capabilities you absolutely need to succeed.
- List all the things you do that add customer value.
- Make sure that you do your financial homework.
- Imagine several different versions of your company's future.

Business Success Based on Six Factors

A combination of several fundamental factors determines the success of a business. Refer to the following important points to make sure that you are covering all vital areas:

- **Plans:** Company mission, vision, goals, and objectives that all work together.
- **Organization:** A structure for your company that makes sense.
- **Procedures:** Efficient and effective ways of doing things.
- **Leadership:** An ability to influence and

encourage others around you.

- **Skills:** The talents and expertise your people need to succeed.
- **Culture:** Beliefs and attitudes that lead to doing the right thing.

http://www.dummies.com/how-to/content/business-success-based-on-six-factors.html

What Goes into a Business Plan?

A business plan is a key document communicating the developmental objectives of your business. To be sure that this vital information is as functional, accurate and comprehensive as possible, be sure to include the following basics:

- Executive summary
- Company overview
- Business environment
- Company description
- Company strategy
- Financial review
- Action plan

How to Avoid Business Trouble: Eight Key Rules

A dangerous area of marketing arises when people try to bypass regulations that ensure fair pricing, safety, and honest advertising. In the UK, as in Europe and North America, there are regulations as well as self-regulatory industry guidelines:

- Always make sure your pricing is fair to the customers and competitors (because unfair competitive practices are usually illegal).

- Always clarify the limits of warranties for services or goods.

- Always provide full warnings and details about your product's content and source on labels.

- Always follow an open and honest policy with the media.

- Never say anything deceptive or misleading in ads or other communications – remember the watchwords 'legal, decent, honest, and truthful'.

- Never distribute products that can do significant harm to anyone.

- Never discuss prices with competitors (that's called price fixing).
- Always keep an eye on future trends that could impact on your performance.

http://www.dummies.com/how-to/content/how-to-avoid-business-trouble-eight-key-rules.html

Sample Business Plans from Bplans.com

Browse this library of sample business plans, provided by Bplans.com. You'll find plans from industries such as restaurants, health care, retail and more.

You can create plans like these using LivePlan business planning software.

The business plans here were originally published on Bplans.com and have been re-published here with permission.

Categories

Airline and Aviation 4 free plans
Bar and Nightclub 7 free plans
Beauty Salon and Day Spa 3 free plans
Bed and Breakfast and Hotel 2 free plans
Car Wash and Automotive 10 free plans
Coffee Shop and Internet Cafe 7 free plans

Computer Consulting, Repair, and Reseller 8 free plans
Construction and Engineering 5 free plans
Consulting 7 free plans
Day Care Services and Children's Products 3 free plans
Education and Training 7 free plans
Farm and Food Production 5 free plans
Fitness Center, Golf Course, and Sports 7 free plans
Home Business 12 free plans
Magazine Publishing and Media Communications 2 free plans
Manufacturing 14 free plans
Medical and Health Care 7 free plans
Nonprofit 2 free plans
Personal Services 23 free plans
Pet Services and Products 3 free plans
Product Development 2 free plans
Professional Services 14 free plans
Real Estate 3 free plans
Recycling and Waste Management 1 free plan
Restaurant, Cafe, and Bakery 22 free plans
Retail and Online Store 19 free plans
Wedding and Event Planning 2 free plans
Wholesale and Distributor 12 free plans

http://www.entrepreneur.com/

Is Your Product or Service Marketable

- Envision yourself as the client or customer that's purchasing your product.
- Would you be happy with it?
- Would you tell your friends and family about it?
- Would you come back to spend more money for it?
- Is the quality of the service or product satisfying?

These are things the client or customer is looking for! So before you launch your business make sure you can answer all those questions and more, with no doubt in your heart. I don't want to discourage you or cause you to over think your business. I just want you to be honest with yourself before others; rather it's good or bad. It's better to reflect on what you have to offer so you can perfect it.

Your Dreams and Visions Will Only Become Reality When You Work Them, Believe Them and Become Them.

April D Williams

Face Your Fears, Persevere Through Your Struggles and Jump Over Your Obstacles

April D Williams

Resources

Here are all the websites I listed throughout this book. Use them on as needed bases. If you decide to pay for a membership on any test them out first. And make sure it's the right time to use them. I wasted a lot of money paying before needing.

Legal Documentation and Contracts

https://www.rocketlawyer.com

http://www.legalcontract.com/

http://formswift.com/

Important Business Sites Study

http://www.SBA.gov

http://www.dnb.com/

www.bbb.org

https://www.uschamber.com/

Microsoft Office Free Templates.

https://templates.office.com/Templates

Logo Building websites

http://www.freelogoservices.com/

http://www.logogarden.com/

http://www.creativemarket.com

http://www.cooltext.com/logos

Online Printing stores for all your marketing and advertising materials.

http://www.uprinting.com/

http://www.vistaprint.com/

http://www.avery.com/avery/en_us/

Great Fee Website Building Platforms.

www.wix.com

http://www.weebly.com

www.homestead.com

http://www.web.com

Freelance Virtual Help and Virtual-Assistants

http://www.fiverr.com

http://www.odesk.com/Virtual-Assistants

http://www.answerconnect.com

http://www.virtualassistantfromphilippines.com

Social Pages Sites

www.YouTube.com

www.FaceBook.com

www.Twitter.com

www.meetup.com

www.linkedin.com

www.istagram.com

Great time management website.

www.rescuetime.com

Please note some of these recommended sites are Affiliates. However, I find them to be of great use to my colleagues and I. If you find the websites can aid in your success, I would appreciate if you would signup through my affiliates links. The small commissions helps me to keep my books and website available to continue giving you needed information for your entrepreneur journey.

http://chroniclesoflivin.com/resources/

http://chroniclesoflivin.com/helpful-links/

http://chroniclesoflivin.com/how-to/

Last Tips and Reminders

Create productive daily routines and be consistent with it.

Stop procrastinating, you are not promised tomorrow so write out your plans and goals, set dates and times and stick to them.

Cut the distractions out! This is your life and time so when distractions come your way take a deep breath and be honest with yourself; "Is the distraction really something that needs your attention right now?" Is it the usual family drama, gossiping phone call? Is it that needy person that always needs you to come to the rescue? Or that favorite TV show that you feel you just can't miss? You get the point; all these things will continue to hinder our dreams, purpose and visions if we allow them to. Those people and TV shows will still be there when you complete your goals one at a time.

When obstacles come into play, which they will; do not stress out. Worrying and Stress causes cloudy thoughts and bad decisions. Take a moment pray about it, meditate, take a long hot candle light bath, or go get a massage. Better yet just simply encourage someone else that's going through a trial or tribulation in his or her life. That always keeps me humble. Bottom line there is always someone in a worst position then you are. Do all you can and trust God to do the rest the situation will never change because you are stressed out or worrying yourself to death! Keep a clear head when dealing with obstacles, struggles and problems. Speaking from experience, you will be able to look at the issues in different angles and almost always find another way around them.

Be open to change and advice, never be a know it all. You can miss out on some vital information and lose great potential relationships. Just because your way has been working in your eyes, someone can come along and take your life or business to a level you could never imagine. Their one little piece of advice can be a major key to your success!

Always be grateful to God and people that support and help you. A prideful and egotistical attitude is not cute! It can push away possible help or clients.

Always present your self in a professional manner. Keep a respectful image and good hygiene.

Keep up with your daily logs of spending and To-Dos. Keep good notes of purchase confirmations, names, and conversation times and dates. The more organized you are the more control you will have and less mistakes you will make.

Follow up with all contacts you meet, they might not be able to help you but they might know someone who can.

Go the extra mile for your clients; word of mouth is the most powerful marketing tool for promotion. Remember people talk!

Don't expect things to happen overnight, it takes patients, time and hard work for long term success.

Most of all get your life and mentality in order before you start your entrepreneur journey. This doesn't mean your credit has to be totally "A1" perfect or you have to have an abundance of money in the bank. It means, get rid of distractions, have your spirit in check, be ready to focus, have your credit repair in process and saving plan in place. Also have your daily routine, planned goals and attitude on GO!

For Life Coaching, Startup Business Consulting or Web design visit:

http://www.lifecoaching2live.com

I look forward to meeting you!:)

Habakkuk 2 New King James Version (NKJV)

The Just Live by Faith

2 Then the Lord answered me and said:

"Write the vision

And make it plain on tablets,

That he may run who reads it.

3 For the vision is yet for an appointed time;

But at the end it will speak, and it will not lie.

Though it tarries, wait for it;

Because it will surely come,

It will not tarry.

4 "Behold the proud,

His soul is not upright in him;

But the just shall live by his faith.

https://www.biblegateway.com/

To support my teenage son's books as well - Please visit:

Amazon.com/author/zamirdeonwilliams

Thanks in Advance For Your Support!

Until The Next Book

Value yourself, your time and know your worth!

April D Williams

"HAVE A HAPPY ENTREPRENEURSHIP"

Lessons I Learned As An Entrepreneur

How I Can Save You From Costly Mistakes

By April D Williams

http://www.chroniclesoflivin.com

An imprint of LyfeLyne Enterprize LLC

Disclaimer: This book was written from my experiences with life, entrepreneurship and industries I worked in. My advice is suggested from results I have witnessed. Neither LyfeLyne Enterprize LLC nor I am responsible for any business conducted with third party companies through the advice or suggestions in this book. Please ask questions and read all provided third party links terms for your self when deciding what will be in the best interest for you and your company.

www.ingramcontent.com/pod-product-compliance
Lightning Source LLC
Chambersburg PA
CBHW020016050426
42450CB00005B/492